HONEY BADGER

BADGER

DON'T CARE™

Andrews McMeel Publishing, LLC
an Andrews McMeel Universal company
1130 Walnut Street, Kansas City, Missouri 64106

www.andrewsmcmeel.com

11 12 13 14 15 RR6 10 9 8 7 6 5 4 3 2 1

ISBN: 978-1-4494-1965-3

Library of Congress Control Number: 2011937528

www.randallsanimals.com

Book design by Diane Marsh

Love the Crazy Nastyass Honey Badger? Play the game, "Honey Badger Don't Care!" Available for iPhone and Android.

ATTENTION: SCHOOLS AND BUSINESSES
Andrews McMeel books are available at quantity discounts with bulk purchase for educational, business, or sales promotional use. For information, please e-mail the Andrews McMeel Publishing Special Sales Department: specialsales@amuniversal.com

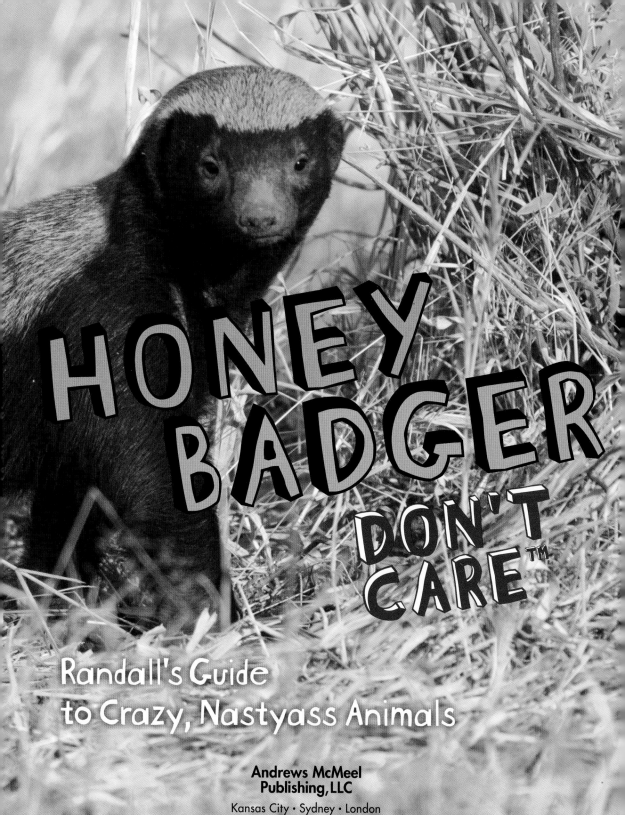

HONEY BADGER

DON'T CARE™

Randall's Guide
to Crazy, Nastyass Animals

**Andrews McMeel
Publishing, LLC**

Kansas City • Sydney • London

CONTENTS

HONEY BADGER DON'T CARE

BY KEITH AND COLLEEN BEGG

FOR MORE THAN TWO DECADES the sheer charisma of the "crazy nastyass" honey badger has fascinated us. Many thousands of hours spent living with wild honey badgers has left us in awe of these wonderful critters and their fearless attitude. But how do we capture the peculiar spirit of these creatures and share it with the world? As researchers, filmmakers, and conservationists, we try to build a relationship between people and a specific species in the hopes that this might develop greater conservation awareness. We believe strongly that people cannot care about an animal they know nothing about. Often we feel like we are preaching to the converted. The people who watch the documentaries and read the articles or scientific papers on badgers and other amazing critters are already convinced about the value of conservation and biodiversity.

But then came Randall! Nothing could have ever prepared us for the unexpected Internet phenomenon that Randall unleashed on millions of animal lovers through YouTube. Randall has done what we could not. He has grabbed the attention of audiences through creature comedy, capturing the imaginations of millions of viewers that mainstream media typically misses out on. His refreshingly unconventional "badass" approach has created a groundswell of badger fever, as nastyass goes viral around the world. In this hilarious read, Randall and assistant Christopher Gordon expose us to 10 even more intriguing and bizarre creatures that are all very real animals. This is better than fiction.

Most of Randall's creatures face a precarious future. Honey badgers, despite their formidable and tenacious character, are disappearing from former ranges with ever increasing persecution and habitat loss. All seven billion of us are responsible for the futures of the aye-aye, the pink fairy armadillo, the tarsier, and the solenodon . . . to mention but a few. Now that your curiosity has been piqued, we urge you to go and discover more about these creatures and get involved in their conservation. What an amazing, wonderful world it is out there. Let's keep it that way. Honey badgers don't care, but we should.

Introduction

Oh, hello there! Allow me to introduce myself: I'm Randall. Most folksies out there know me as the voice behind the Internet sensation "The Crazy Nastyass Honey Badger," and why not? The video is pretty fantabulous, if I do say so myself! Peace, love, and the protection and care for animals, through education and comedy: That is my mission. Life is too short, lovies—and as you know, **many animals and people need our help.** Together, we can make this world a better place to live!

Love,
Randall =)
X O X O

What a little **badass!**

THE
HONEY BADGER

(Crazy nastyass)

THIS . . . IS THE HONEY BADGER. Otherwise known as "the crazy nastyass"! Looks like he's saying, "Oh, hi, sweetie, I didn't see ya there." Right? Well think again, stupid. This honey badger's vicious as fuck, and *will* bite your balls off. You think I'm kidding? Well, I'm not! Honey badger don't give a shit.

The honey badger's been referred to by *The Guinness Book of World Records* as "the most fearless animal in all the animal kingdom." It really doesn't give a shit. What a little badass! Unfortunately, as of late, they've had to deal with human opposition, but are thankfully being protected in some of their habitats. Found predominately in South Africa, parts of the Middle East, and Southeast Asia, they can also be found in Morocco and Algeria, as well as along the Indian peninsula. I just love that while you're on a fabulous vacation you could possibly run into a honey badger!

OMFG—Did this honey badger get her claws did? How fierce!

EwW, my Jesus, Mary, Joseph and the Technicolor Dream Coat—so gross, look—it's eating a mouse!

GO AHEAD, SMARTY. JUST TRY and think of another animal that gives less of a shit than this little beast. You can't! Even bears and lions feel bad every once in a while! But not the honey badger! In fact, this no-nonsense rudey-pants has no known predators! It does, however, have a long list of nastyass snacks: larvae and other items found in a house full of bees; cobras, puff adders, and other venomous snakes; mongooses; rodents; lion's balls; elephant ass—I mean, seriously, must I go on with the world's most nauseating grocery list? When not eating meats, it'll snack on berries, various fruits, and some veggies. But, let's face it, those times are rare!

NOW, WHILE THE HONEY BADGER is snacking away, other animals—sneaky wild jackals and carnivorous birds—like to hang around and pretend they're minding their own business. That is, until the honey badger's done eating. Then they swoop in to pick up the scraps! They say, "You do all the work for us, honey badger, and we'll just eat whatever you find, how's that? What do you say, stupid?" Sometimes, even a lion will try to moochy-mooch off of a honey badger! Look at this crazy shit between a lion and honey badger over snacksies!

OMG—do you see the size of this honey badger's testicles?!

No wonder they don't care—their balls are the size of fresh cantaloupes!

Q. **DO YOU KNOW WHAT A "RATEL" IS?**

A. No, stupid, it's not a "French rat"—it's another name for the honey badger! Males are referred to as "boars" (sillycakes) and females as "sows" (silliercakes!). Boars are about a foot tall and two and a half feet long. They weigh between 25 and 36 pounds. Sows weigh between 20 and 22 pounds at the most.

Q. **DID YOU KNOW THAT HONEY BADGERS ARE NOCTURNAL?**

A. When the sun goes down, the honey badger hits the town for some extreme hunting! They're fabulous climbers, and will run up trees to knock down animals and eat them! They'll climb right up there all lickity-splits to ravage a bird's house for chicks and eggs, or to smack some snakes around!

BY NOW, I THINK YOU get the idea—no animal is safe from the honey badger. It doesn't matter where these other animals live—the honey badger must keep eating and always gets what it wants! Honey badgers have recently been under attack by beekeepers who are sick of their hives getting destroyed, their honey stolen. Efforts have been made to protect the honey badgers from their out-for-blood human enemies. However, as beekeepers have learned, it is extremely difficult to kill a honey badger! Because it's so powerful and has such thick skin, the honey badger's body is very hard to penetrate. Arrows, machetes, bites, stings, stabs—even fucking bullets—won't do much. You have to attack a honey badger's head in order to put it down . . . good luck with that one, stupid!

Look, you can tell this honey badger's up to no good! See its thick skin and fabulous coat?

PROTECTED IN INDIA, THIS NASTYASS is actually related to the wolverine. That is one family reunion I can skip! Could you imagine? "Hey, Henry, can you pass the elephant ass? "Suuure! I'll trade you for those lion's balls?" No thank you!!!

In captivity, honey badgers may live up to 24 years; out in the wild, about half as long.

OK, LET'S TALK ABOUT SEX . . . HONEY badger sex! While honey badgers *do* indeed have sex (obvi), the "when and how" is unclear! They're very modest, and have yet to allow any outsiders to observe their mating habits (except for Colleen and Keith Begg, who studied honey badgers for many years over in the Kalahari). The female will usually walk around and leave behind sexy odors to let all the honey badger boys know she's "looking for a good time"! And soon enough, horny male honey badgers will stop by her burrow, unannounced! She chooses one male to make passionate love with, and before you know it they have a cub (or "kit") together. And in the tradition of not giving a shit, the boar will leave only after a few days with his new family, to move on with his life! Some nerve! Meanwhile, the single sow mother is responsible for showing baby the ropes.

BABY HONEY BADGERS ARE BORN blind and haven't much time to get used to everything, what with all the lions and tigers around. Adult honey badgers have no predators, but their little babies are always at risk.

A GOOD HONEY BADGER MOTHER will teach her kit to dig, cool off with sand baths, and, ultimately, to hunt. If the baby can't keep up, the mother will drag its ass down into a burrow to hide it while she begrudgingly gets them food on her own. She'll work quickly, knowing nasty, carnivorous predators are waiting for a tasty baby snack!

Oh, holy sh♥t! That lioness has just stolen that poor li'l honey badger baby! Look how floppy and innocent it looks!

Q. DID YOU KNOW IN ADDITION TO BEING SO BADASS, HONEY BADGERS ARE ALSO EXTREMELY INTELLIGENT?

A. In fact they're one of the few species out there in this wild, wild world of ours that uses tools! Isn't that precious? They use logs, rocks, branches, and all kinds of crazy shit to get what they want! Fabulous!

Look how smart this honey badger is! Is he giving a lecture at Yale?

HONEY BADGERS HAVE LITTLE DOGGIELIKE muzzles to go with their sharpass canine teeth! Folks think they're cute based on their name and their adorable dog-meets-badger body, but, let's face it—they're fucking nuts.

This is Eshe and Shani from the Naples Zoo, in Florida. Look how much they adore each other's company! There's no question, these two are the Thelma and Louise of honey badgers!

But who says honey badgers can't be affectionate? Take a look here. For the first time ever caught on film, two female honey badgers are being so snuggly! Looks like these two have been through everything together! How splendid! If these walls could talk (or in this case, "if this dirt and mouse poo could talk")!

"Listen, dear," says Shani, "would you mind rubbing my neck? It is killing me today for some stupid reason!"

"Of course!" proclaims Eshe, and there she goes, rubbing her friend's neck and getting out those hard-to-reach honey badger knots!

"You wanna watch something later?"

"Sure," says Eshe. "I just DVR'd Digging with the Stars!"

HONEY BADGERS LOVE ROLLING AROUND in mud and dirt puddles. They get so nasty and filthy! I bet they would have loved Woodstock!

Looks like this honey badger just wants to take a li'l power nap in the sand. You know, a li'l sleepy time— wake me in 20, and I'll be good to go!

HERE'S A HONEY BADGER JUST chillin' up in its crib and deciding what to wear before going out hunting. As you can see, the pad is kind of small—a bit cramped—but sooooooo cozy! And it's rent controlled! Fabulous!!!

LOOK—THIS HONEY BADGER DOESN'T know whether to roll over and pass the fuck out from exhaustion or just go hunting! "Maybe I should dig up some rodents . . ." he muses. Decisions, decisions, huh? Ah, such is life for the honey badger. You probably already noticed their sweet little ears. Pretty cool, if you ask me. They're close to their heads so they don't get hurt in battles or while digging.

Oh, hello there, honey badger!

WHAT CAN I SAY? THEY'RE all a dash of cute and a whole lotta nasty! The mothers do a terrific job of raising their kits, yet the fathers are deadbeats. As crazy and nastyass as they may be, honey badgers have certainly taught us humans a lot. You know what? They should start breeding them to become motivational speakers! I bet they'd do so well! Everyone would certainly listen!

li'l freaky thang!

THE AYE-AYE

(What the fuck?!)

THIS IS . . . FUCKING *TERRIFYING* IS what it is! This is the aye-aye, or, as I like to call it, "the li'l freaky thang"! As you can see from the pictures, this little wannabe lemur is quite the looker! I don't get it—did Don Knotts fuck a bat?

Good grief! This is, like, really starting to freak me out!

Look at these two! Don knotts fucked a bat!

THE AYE-AYE CAN BE FOUND in Madagascar's rain forests as well as in some sleazy nightclubs throughout the United States! Sadly, stupid logging and farming is slowly killing off this freaky li'l wonder baby. Conservation is key in the recovery of this species. More and more is thankfully being done to protect the **endangered/near-threatened** aye-aye.

"Can I give you a hand?"

"No—uh . . . no, thank you, aye-aye!"

LOOK AT ITS NASTY LI'L HANDS! Yuck! Boneyass freaks are what they are! According to legend, aye-ayes are like Madagascar's grim reaper and represent death! Why am I so not surprised? Just look at their hands! Imagine shaking that hand? I mean, how can you even look one in the eye during a conversation? Forget it! Serious efforts should be made to get these freaky li'l fucks some sunglasses and gloves!

In addition to the endless destruction of its habitat, the aye-ayes' numbers have dwindled due to superstition. See, people think they're bad luck—especially if they point their longass middle finger at you. Out of fear, aye-ayes are killed to "break death's spell." Are you kidding me? Spells? Legends?

Q. AND WHAT EXACTLY IS THIS LI'L FREAK?

A. It's funny I should ask: It's, like, a bit of a primate with a dash of rodent. Gross combo, *riiight?*! But you see, stupid, ever since Frenchy nature lover Louis-Jean-Marie Daubenton discovered it eons ago, *not one person* has been able to say exactly what this freak is! Even a platypus has an identity! I repeat: No one knows what exactly the fuck the aye-aye is! It is popular belief that it's a type of primate—but what kind? Prosimian? Indriidae? Well, while everyone out there continues to argue over what this thing is, I will continue to be freaked out by its fucked-up face. Good Mary Lou, this is a tough little creature to write about. Not only does it scare the shit outta me, but there is just not that much known about this little fucker.

Is it just me, or does it look a little bit cute here? Wait, forget it! I'm scared!

HERE ARE SOME THINGS I do know. Aye-ayes love to spend a lot of their time up in trees, just, you know, swinging and dancing around. They love to snack on some gross shit, including animal poop and insect larvae! *Ewww!* That is so nasty, right?!

Crazyface here also eats nuts and fruits, like coconuts and mangoes. They also eat various insects, including beetles, which they love—but, hey—who isn't a beetles fan?

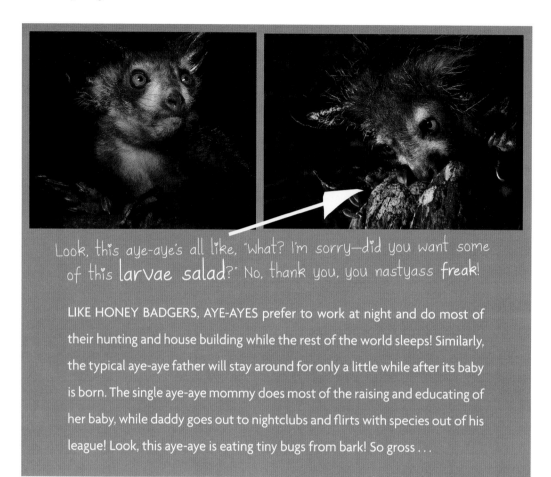

Look, this aye-aye's all like, "What? I'm sorry—did you want some of this **larvae salad**?" No, thank you, you nastyass **freak**!

LIKE HONEY BADGERS, AYE-AYES prefer to work at night and do most of their hunting and house building while the rest of the world sleeps! Similarly, the typical aye-aye father will stay around for only a little while after its baby is born. The single aye-aye mommy does most of the raising and educating of her baby, while daddy goes out to nightclubs and flirts with species out of his league! Look, this aye-aye is eating tiny bugs from bark! So gross . . .

THESE FREAKY BABIES WILL WEIGH up to four pounds and can reach as tall as two feet. *Waittt*, I thought they were way smaller than that! It'd be like walking around town with E.T.! The aye-aye prefers to live alone, but every now and then one of them will meet its soul mate and the sparks fly! Maybe some smarty out there will start www.aye-date.com for all those lonely singles!

AYE-AYES HAVE HUGE BUSHY TAILS, and as you can see, largeass crazy peepers to go along with their big, sensitive ears that help them hear when li'l snacks and treats are walking around. Since most of their time is spent staying up all night, they ball up and sleep all day. Sounds like me in the '80s! Oh, dear! They are considered the largest nocturnal primate.

FYI: Aye-ayes love rain forests and tend to chill in homes they've created from leaves, twigs, and other branchy things. When the lunch bell rings, they use their longass "death" middle fingers to scoop out nasty larvae and bugs from the trees. Ugh—anyway.

Oh, God—what the hell is it licking there?! Nasty! Is it . . . is it licking up insects and nasty shit off that tree? **Gag me!**

Too much eyeliner, darling . . . it looks like you just escaped from rehab, OK?

ODDLY, AYE-AYES HAVE A DENTAL record that reads more like a rodent's than a primate's. They have nasty, sharp little incisor teeth, which, strangely enough, grow throughout their lives! You couldn't pay me enough to be an aye-aye dentist! Good mercy, could you imagine that bullshit? Although they're so outgoing around humans, sadly, often, when they go into town, they spook people out, and get themselves killed! It's horrible.

Friend of
satan!

THE TASMANIAN DEVIL

(Satan's best friend)

FIRST OFF, HOLY SHIT! You see those crazy devil teeth?! The Tasmanian devil lives in Tasmania (duh!), an Aussie island state rich in both its nature and beauty! Back in the day, these nasty devils were found all over Australia, but then became extinct. This was in large part due to the dingo (which apparently stole more than

"We'll come out to play, but then we'll have to **bite** your face, OK?"

just babies)! Even though it was mostly these dingoes stealing and eating farmers' livestock, the poor Tasmanian devils got the blame and, tragically, many were killed off by senseless hunters. Then, around the late '90s, a terrible and crazy disease known as "devil facial tumor disease" caused their numbers to dwindle even more! Conservation and scientific efforts are being made to help save this **endangered** nastyass friend of Satan.

NOW, TAKE A LOOK AT this devil's back foot and you'll notice it has four toes with claws that never retract—they just, like, stay there, ready to scratch shit up! Wait—have I mentioned they're marsupials? It's true, and, presently, they're Australia's largest meat-eating marsupial! So take that, you fluffyass, vegan kangaroos!

OH, MY FUCKING SHITCAKES, please have mercy! Can you believe this devil?! It's just snacking away on a poor little . . . what is that? Is that a wallaby? You see, they eat all sorts of nasty shit—from little mice to wombats and sheep! Satan's best friend also enjoys eating large leftover scraps—mainly dead buried animals. There's an old folktale that, once upon a time, a gross Tasmanian Satan helper dug its way into a buried horse's resting place and ate its poor lifeless body! Oh Jesus.

WHEN THESE DEVILS SENSE DANGER or get stressed out, they release a gross, disgusting
odor, which basically lets everyone know,

Yeah, I farted. You know . . . I'm stressed, what do you want from me?

Meanwhile, look at this pack of devils enjoying a little snacking party! How horrid . . . seriously!

LEGEND HAS IT THAT WHEN two European settlers arrived in Australia, one turned to
the other and asked, "Did you fart, Ernie?" And Ernie was like, "Whoever smelt it, dealt
it." This debate went on for hours until they discovered nearby a little freak shaking
his little body from utter rage and releasing potent anal vapors! And that's how it got
its name, the Tasmanian devil. You see, when the devils feel threatened, in addition
to releasing their gross anal vapors, they act wild—growling, snarling, attacking, and
showing their sharp teeth!

Holy shit.
I think I left
my keys in
the carcass!

TASMANIAN DEVILS ARE NOCTURNAL. THEY stay up all night hunting for snacks, and by midafternoon they're sunbathing comfortably and gossiping with friends about last night's roadkill. You know what else? When they eat, they eat it all—bones, fur, flesh. No scraps!

Oh my goodness!
Holy—what the?! This
devil's angry as hell
or yawning—regardless,
I think I just peed
myself a little bit!

fact-tastic: Tasmanian devils have a nice, furry black coat and are built like Jack Russell weight lifters! These satanic dogs store fat in their tails, and you can always tell a healthy devil by how chubs its tail is! Now, that is kind of cute, I have to say!

which elementary school
is right for your devil?

Q. **DID YOU KNOW HOW THEY MAKE BABIES?**

A. You won't believe this: OK, so devils are in no way monogamous! However, if a male's, like, really, *really* into his mate, he'll stick around and help raise the pups in the den. And the next time mama devil is ovulating, the same male will be there to make more pups! A female usually gives birth to up to 30 pups! Not only that, but she stands up while giving birth! Despite her huge litters, mama has only four nipples, so the precious pups take turns nursing in her pouch. Meanwhile, papa reads the paper and kills mice!

"Next Fall, everyone will be wearing one of these, stupid!"

WHILE EFFORTS HAVE BEEN MADE to save this wild species from total extinction, it's been very hard to do, what with the introduction of the cancerous "devil facial tumor disease" and constant hunting and killing. There's no doubt about it, stupid, that zoos are proving instrumental in their protection and longevity!

Although **endangered**, the Tasmanian devil remains the symbol of the Tasmanian Parks and Wildlife Service, and serves as a popular icon throughout Australia. Hopefully, this nasty li'l devil will remain for generations to come.

Captain
Sellecks

THE EMPEROR TAMARIN

(Mustacheous groomy)

NOW, I KNOW WHAT YOU'RE asking: "Randall, what the fuck is that crazy-looking man (with the fabulous mustache) doing in your book on crazy, nastyass animals?" Well, stupid, although it may look like a wild man, it's really an emperor tamarin! It's a fabulous primate that dwells in the lovely rain forests and tree-dense areas of Brazil and Peru. It gets its name from the last emperor of Germany and king of Prussia, Kaiser Wilhelm II, to whom it bears an uncanny resemblance!

Will you look at that?! Do my eyes deceive me? Am I seeing double?

THE EMPEROR TAMARIN LOVES TO snack on sap, sweet nectars, fruits, flowers, and—oh my sweet goodness, will you look at that little body?! That mustache is so precious!

These dapper li'l primates, which usually live about 17 years, measure up to around 10 to 11 inches when standing. They take great pride in their perfect mustaches—even the ladies! And why not? Their fur and mustache hairs are fabulous and require extra attention! In fact, they bond with one another through their grooming sessions! Sounds familiar! Oh, the gossip they must have!

Mmmm, delish! Thanks for the grape, stupid!

This picture makes me want a grape . . . seriously

THESE "CAPTAIN SELLECKS," as I like to call 'em, live in groups usually consisting of one or two females and three or four males. When babies are born, everybody takes turns caring for them, including the males! Finally! As you've probably noticed, some nastyass male animals don't give a shit about their babies! How rude! Listen, just because you bring home an antelope ass for dinner doesn't mean you get to jump ship once your baby is about to walk! Anyway, kudos to these Captain Sellecks for helping their women raise the babies, while successfully proving hippie commune living is still alive!

Awww, why so glum, chum? Did someone take your grapes, li'l emperor? Cheer up, stupid. Listen, at least your fur and mustache look fabulous . . . am I right?

NOW AND THEN, THESE CAPTAIN SELLECKS will shout at the top of their li'l lungs to let everyone know their whereabouts—how thoughtful, yet crazy, right? These sweet little babies play all day and are in bed by about ten at night. What good primates!

Look at how those pretty black hands and feet perfectly complement his beautiful fur and mustache!

pink and cutesy

THE PINK FAIRY ARMADILLO

(Outrageously shelly)

ASIDE FROM BEING THE MOST fascinating and outrageous member of the armadillo family, the pink fairy is also the family's smallest species, with a length (from the nose to the start of its tail) of about five inches! How adorable! It is also the only member of the armadillo fam to have its shell almost completely separated from its li'l body. Found in Argentina and parts of South America, throughout plains and grasslands, this special pink fairy armadillo is, sadly, classified as an **endangered** species. Due to both changes to its habitat and being hunted by nasty wild and domestic dogs, its numbers have dwindled. But more and more people are starting to adopt them as pets, which is great on the one hand, but I just hope they get the proper care and attention they deserve!

These flamboyant armadillos love to stay up all night just snacking on ants, digging dirt, and sexting random animals! They're just so crazy outrageous! Look at this one's pink li'l nose! How precious!

"I may be pink and cutesy, but I'm also a survivor and don't have to take any of your shit, stupid!"

Hey—did someone forget their purse? Or is that a hat? OMG . . . is that a broach? **How fancy!** *Shhhh, this pink fairy needs her* **sleepy time!**

THEY ARE MASTER DIGGERS AND love to dig their burrows. When scared or threatened, they can completely bury themselves for protection within seconds! No jokes! Look, they're not stupid: They know they're on the brink of extinction— they must do whatever it takes to survive and go about their business without incident!

THIS PICTURE SHOULD GIVE YOU a good idea of how marvelously tiny these armadillos are. See how rosy pink and special they are?! Mostly, when the average idiot thinks of an armadillo, they only visualize a helmet with feet, or the armadillo running all over the place in the Clash's music video for their big folk song "Rock the Casbah"! Do you remember that classic hit? Oh, I do.

AS YOU CAN ALSO SEE, its little pink hand-paws, are perfect for digging. And dig it does—for food, shelter, babies, sexytimes, cooling off—you name it! Because its protective armor is not so-so attached, it has a great deal of mobility with regards to its body—it can move about freely, knowing its fabulous armor is both protective yet loose.

I just think their white hair is ab-fabulous! Look how pretty nature has made these little armadillos! They truly are the roses of the armadillo fam.

Q. HERE, YOU CAN SEE THE LI'L PINK SHELLY'S TAIL. SEE HOW IT'S KINDA DRAGGING BACK THERE?

A. That's because the pink fairy is incapable of raising its little tail! Its bone plate at the butt end of the armor is fucking attached to its pelvic area! Can you believe that shit?!

PINK FAIRIES ARE LONERS UNTIL they meet their mates! Isn't that sweet? They make babies and the females give birth to usually four pups—all identical! How the hell can they tell them apart?!

A pup is born with a soft, leathery plate that eventually hardens into its protective armor as it gets older . . . kind of like some people I know! Perhaps there's some way we can employ these little pink fairies as oil diggers? Is that a crazy idea? You never know. If it helps create pink fairy jobs and prolongs their species, then it sounds grand to me! In the meantime, in captivity, the pink fairy can live up to 15 years. Efforts are continuing to save this crazy, precious, and beautiful armadillo species.

LOOK AT ME— I'M RICH!

sappy
funmuffins

THE
TARSIER

(Little crazyface)

WELL, I DON'T KNOW WHAT more to tell you about the tarsier you couldn't already tell from its picture, so I'll just be over here . . . ha, ha, ha! Psych! Oh, stop it, I'm just pulling your chain—trust me, there's a lot to know about this wild little crazyface! For starters, if you guessed it was a primate, you are correct! If you guessed it was something else, you're stupid! These babies are nocturnal—I guess so they can make use of those headlights where their eyes should be! They dwell in the Philippines, Borneo, and Indonesia—basically the fabulous Southeast Asian islands. Gorgeous! Sadly, once again, the tarsier and its cousins (subspecies and whonot), despite having an impressive 45 million year run, are now either **threatened and/or endangered.**

The tarsier is shy. Its behavior around us humans is based on paranoia and skepticism. In fact, too often, attempts to domesticate tarsiers will end horribly in suicide. Can you fucking believe it? I mean—what? That's just horrible, but true based on actual incidents: If tarsiers are depressed and miserable enough in their newly controlled environments, they will find a way to kill themselves. So, now you know—do not drastically change this little crazyface's habitat, bring it home, and expect it to sit and roll over for you! Nothing like an overdramatic, misunderstood endangered species to cheer you up, right? Jesus . . .

LET ME TELL YOU ABOUT their gigantic eyes! I mean, those peepers have probably seen it all! Each eye's got a diameter of roughly 16 to 18 millimeters. Let's just hope one of them doesn't need bifocal contact lenses anytime soon.

Oh, have I mentioned how it got its name? Would you care to guess? Oh, enough of that stupid guessing shit; look: The tarsier gets its name from the "tarsus," which is, at the end of the night, simply a group of bones in the foot. However, theirs are super crazy long! So some "smarty" was all like, "*Ooooh*, I know—let's call it a 'tarsier,' since its tarsus is sooo long!" "Sappy Funmuffins," "Furry Eye-Monkey," and "The Burrito" were some failed suggestions. "The Tarsier" stuck. But remember, this li'l primate's cousins had been around long before it was even given a name!

Well, look at Triparooni Jones over here! This li'l guy looks like he took so much ecstasy he ain't never gonna come down!

HOLY SHIT! DID YOU JUST read that nasty photo convo?! That is so nasty, but true! Tarsiers are indeed carnivores and love to snack on live animals, including birds! And they really eat *all* of the bird—feathers, beak, even its fucking feet! Are you cereal? That is so nasty! Poor birds. Crazy tarsiers! They also love to snack on lizards, snakes, moths, beetles, and insects.

With their large eyes and somewhat aggressive territorial behavior, I bet "Are you looking at me?!" is heard often!

HERE'S SOME INTERESTING INFO FOR you to gnaw on: Tarsiers are territorial and have been known to ward off other horny tarsiers from their mates! True monogamists! Sometimes, they'll form groups and meet up with other groups and go shopping together! No, stupid, they don't actually go *shopping* together, but they might as well since they look for food and shelter in a cute little group anyway.

Territory is very important to these little freaks, so they walk around and spray things with their scent, marking the parameters of their group's camp. Once camp has been set up, they spend a lot of time grooming and snuggling! How precious!

TARSIERS DWELL ALL OVER THE PLACE, from shrubbylands to lush grasslands. To this day, peeps continue to debate their exact classification within the primate family. Oh my goodness, you see how they all come out at night?! They look like little monkey mice or something, right?

WAAAAAHHH-HHAHAHAHA-HAHGGGHHHHH!

TARSIERS ARE ALSO CREATURES OF many voices. They have chirps, whistles, squeaks, and screams to mean all kinds of different shit. So, like, instead of calmly announcing, "Hey, there are some tarsiers we don't know entering our camp," with a shake of a tail or a leap into the air, they're like, "WAAAAAH-HHHHAHAHAHAHAHGGGHHHHH!" They have an extensive secret vocab they use with one another. It's a fabulous way to keep in touch and let every tarsier know what's going on.

Get a load of this chubby tarsier! I'm glad they have this butterball on the lookout! Geez!

ALL TARSIERS ARE BORN WITHOUT siblings—that's right, they're all single children! Tarsier sex lasts only about one to two minutes! But don't let them know I told you that. I mean, they're endangered, shy, and suicidal; the last thing I want for them is to develop some sort of sex complex! The baby tarsiers are born with their eyes wide open! Can you believe that shit?! I would freak out if I were a mama tarsier—to give birth and instantly see your baby look at you with those eyes?! Oh, hell no, stupid!

In addition to being born with their bugged-out eyes already open, they come fur-ready! In fact, fuck it, I'll let you in on a crazy bit of tarsier information . . . you ready? Baby tarsiers are huge, well, compared to their parents! At birth, tarsiers are about two inches long—a little over a quarter of their parents' size! And this is the best part: The mama tarsiers carry around their heavy, largeass babies in their mouths, just like cats! Isn't that outrageous?! But if you ask me, I think this is why they form groups, so a tarsier-sitter can take over while Mommy and Daddy have a special night out . . . eating live birds!

Sex-crazed tarsiers a minute and a half later . . .

Holy shit!
Is that Gollum?
Is that the
'precious ring
of powers' he's
grasping like that?!
What the fuck is
going on here?

I THINK THE TARSIER COULD kick anyone's ass in a staring contest, what do you think? Again, of the eight amazing subspecies of tarsier, a few are presently **endangered** and others are **threatened**. Captivity as an option is hard because of their sensitivity to drastic change. Whether Western, Filipino, or Eastern, there's no doubt about it, stupid, these little crazy-faces are in need of some serious protection to continue to exist.

fucking his

THE OPOSSUM

(Gargoyley hellcat)

WELL, HERE IT IS—THE OPOSSUM. Take a good look at the face of Satan. These little gargoyles scare the shit out of me! I don't know how you, my dear reader, feel about them, but I am absolutely terrified. Is there any reason why I shouldn't be? They fucking hiss! I mean, if you're not a cat or watching bad theater, there's no reason, really, to ever hiss! But they do! It's like the creator of all creatures, great and small, couldn't figure out which way to go with this mammal: "Well, let's make it a new type of cat, no, no, let's make it a cat-rat—yes, yes! A cat-rat that'll terrify anyone with a backyard or an attic!"

This is no laughing matter.
You, opossum, scare the living shit out
of me! Lord, those fucking teeth!

41

fact-tastic:

OK, some things you must know about these nastyass gargoyle hellcats: For starters, they can grab things with their tails, and they have opposable thumbs on their hind feet. Terrifying. It gets better, wait—they're somehow resistant to most major diseases! Are you kidding me? How lucky to be an opossum—no diseases? What the fuck?

NOW, OPOSSUMS ARE ALL OVER the fucking place, but it was the Virginia opossum that really put these marsupial beasts on the map! They're nocturnal, and thank God 'cause, frankly, who the fuck wants to deal with their shit, let alone their faces, during the day? Could you imagine starting every morning with this li'l Satanface at your doorstep? No thanks. Stay sleepless in Seattle, thank you very much! But sometimes, they'll find a way to nestle in your home! I kid you not!

Dear Diary—

One of my dear grandmother's friends, Nelly, had this attic full of, you know, boxes and other attic-y things. Well, one day for no reason, they sent me up there to get some old snuff box. I was around **eight** years old and at the time **had no fear whatsoever of any animal** . . . until I went to go get that stupid snuff box! I climb up there, to the attic, and I'm searching all over the place, and right there—**motionless and silent, with its mouth wide open**—was a fucking opossum, the size of a dresser (or vanity)! Shocked and **scared shitless**, I ran back down, only to be accused of "making up grand tales" 'cause I couldn't find that snuff box! Nelly, I'm eight years old! Why would I lie about a gigantic cat-rat Satan in your stupid attic? I guess I'll save the rest of the story for next week's therapy session! Point being? **Opossums get into fucking everything!**

Truth be told, as nastyass and scary as these opossums are, they really mean no harm whatsoever. In fact, I've learned they're more afraid of us than we are of them (of course, isn't that what they all say?).

NOW, THE HORNY DRIFTER MALES like to walk around making funny noises to attract the ladies. If a female responds . . . chances are it's baby time! Females spawn a bunch of babies, but only a baker's dozen or so will actually survive. You see, once born, opossums must independently find their way into the mama's marsupium (pouch) and to the teat. They'll generally remain in the pouch for a couple of months before braving the real world, when they'll cling onto mama's back for another two months or so—*awww*, look who's all grow'd up now! Still, these opossum mamas prefer their babies learn the ropes as quickly as possible. It's a tough world out there, and for the most part, opossums rarely live long enough to see their fifth birthdays. They do what they can to survive, avoiding cars and other man-made deaths.

No jokes—dipshit here is actually starting a fight with an owl statue. Smooth move, stupid!

SO, MEANWHILE, THE TALES ARE TRUE—when an opossum feels threatened or scared, it will drop and keel over, as though it just died. Thus, "playing possum," and why not? Who wants to deal with some "That's my dead mouse!" drama from another animal or some gigantic humans getting trashed at some stupid backyard party? Sometimes it truly is best to just play dead and let the clouds pass. Then, you can get back up and scare the shit out of someone!

I think the next time I see an opossum I'll play possum first and see if it does the same! Then it'll be a battle of who can play dead the longest.

SINCE OPOSSUMS LOVE TO MAKE crazy noises, including hisses and horny clicks and clacks, I'm thinking maybe they should focus more on singing the hits. You know, do something a little more productive than invading homes and scaring the shit out of people with their gargoyle-lookin' asses! Perhaps this will also help kill the fear I and others have for these nastyass creatures of the night. They can learn to sing, and maybe even record some experimental shit!

"I think Simon was a bit too harsh, as usual, but the others really enjoyed it! You're going to Hollywood!"

THERE'S NO DOUBT ABOUT IT, stupid, opossums are nasty as hell and scare the shit out of me. However, the babies are kind of cute, and every now and then you'll see an opossum that'll steal your heart. But let's face it, those times are few and far between.

THE
SOLENODON

(Li'l grumpypants)

THIS . . . IS THE SOLENODON, OR, as I like to call it, "li'l grumpypants," because, as cute as they appear to be, they are *such* little assholes! First off, hello! They're venomous! Yeah. Imagine that. These contemptuous little-big shrews are also insomniacs and stay up all night eating earthworms and squealing! How gross and rude! They complain all the time with their squealing and will bite for no reason . . . sounds like some assholes I know!

The solenodons have venomous saliva, which spills out through their teeth! How nasty! They snack on small reptiles, froggies, insects, and disgusting worms . . . *ewww*! Their snouts are flexible and help them feel out their environments—kinda like cats' whiskers do.

BUT AS NASTY AND VERBALLY annoying as they may be, sadly, these little mammals are an **endangered** species—no thanks in large part to the ruthless small Asian mongoose. These nasty mongooses were used eons ago to kill rodents, snakes, and crazy homeless cats and dogs! They wound up eating, like, every single little grumpy solenodon! Way to wipe out a species, stupid colonial jerks!

Holy shit! Grumpy much? Clearly, solenodons don't give a shit! Frankly, why should they?

fact-tastic:
In addition to its lovely venomous teeth, the solenodon has these nasty glands that release disgusting odors under its armpits and groin area. Perhaps this is some sort of bizarre defense mechanism? All the more reason to be so fucking rude and grumpy!

Looks like this li'l grumpyass could use a trip to the salon! My Lord, will someone puh-lease call a manicurist, STAT!

ULTIMATELY, WHILE SOLENODONS ARE UNCOORDINATED, semi-defenseless, and neurotic li'l creatures, old uncovered fossils in North America showed they existed nearly 30 million–plus years ago! Imagine—these prehistoric, venomous, grouchy, irritable li'l solenodons walking around with crazy shit we can only see in blockbuster movies! That's survival, honey!

THE SOLENODON'S BODY IS A little over a foot long, and its tail alone is a nasty nine inches. Gross! The remaining species of solenodons can be found in Cuba and Hispaniola, which is a beautiful island made up of the sovereign states of the Dominican Republic and Haiti. These venomous grumpybottoms love to snack on insects and have even been known to eat an occasional lizard or froggy!

Here's a bigass solenodon couple, just looking for some insecty scraps to nibble! Ewwwwww!

THE SOLENODON TENDS TO STAY to itself and is nomadic. The only time it will partner up is when it wants to make babies—which, FYI, happens to be a slowass process. This certainly doesn't improve its endangered status! The typical solenodon mama will give birth to only one litter in any given year, consisting of one to three babies. Now, you're probably asking yourself, "Hey, Randall, is there something unusual about the solenodon mama's teats?" And my answer to your inner question is, "Why, yes! There most certainly is!" The female grumpypants has two teats, and they're on her ass! No jokes! They. Are. On. Her. Buns.

THE MAMAS GIVE BIRTH IN a little nesting burrow that their male counterparts help decorate! It's poop-yer-pants amazing! Mama gets all nice and comfy and has her babies, which'll stay with her until they're young adults, and then leave, without ever looking back! "Thanks, Mom, for your ass-teats. See you later!"

What time's that venomous-saliva party?

THE FIRST RECORDED SIGHTING OF a solenodon dates way the fuck back to, like, 1833. Here's what was happenin' back then: Andy Jackson won a second term as president of the United States, the British Parliament finally got its shit together and passed the Slavery Abolition Act (freeing all of the empire's slaves), a fucking three-year-old became the queen of Spain, the first enzyme was discovered, and on the music charts were the crazy and loud compositions of Chopin, Liszt, and Berlioz! What a crazy fucking time! And right there, in the mix—the solenodon.

Hey, Carol, what time is that fucking anger-management shit supposed to start?!

THESE LITTLE GRUMPY OLD MEN like to violently grunt and scream! We're talking solenodon temper tantrums! God—take a fucking Xanax! They will attack small animals with their venomous bites, so at least they relieve their aggression productively—by getting some snacks!

fact-tastic:

Ain't much has changed for the solenodon in 30 million-plus years. Physically and all that jazz, it's still pretty much the same grumpy asshole that walked beside the pterodactyls! Now that's some deep shit.

MY PAPA USED TO TELL ME a tale of how he saw one once while filming. It was during Halloween—I remember because I was dressed as Rock Hunter and Papa wasn't there (as usual) to see how fabulous I looked. But all was forgiven because he came home with a picture of it for me! I thought he was nuts for taking this picture—knowing it could easily hop at him in a fit of rage and bite his foot or something! But he did it!

A rare and candid photo of a Haitian solenodon on Halloween, taken by Papa in the 1960s. This is a terrible costume, but probably took it hours to make, the poor thing!

FOR WHATEVER REASON, DESPITE BEING venomous, angry, and full of bitterness and rage, when chased by predators, solenodons stop and hide their heads! They're like, "Fuck it, eat me. I'm venomous and grumpy!" Very few remain in captivity, as far as I know. Hopefully, efforts can be made to prolong their existence. It's difficult, though, simply because they really are such li'l bitter assholes! But, again . . . if I had a pair of teats on my ass, I think I'd be bitter, too.

Hello, my name is

Steve

THE WOMBAT

(Li'l Aussie teddy)

THIS . . . IS THE WOMBAT, OR, as I like to call it, "li'l Aussie teddy," because it's native to Australia and looks like a cute li'l teddy bear! Oh, how I want to pick one up and just snuggle the night away! They're not so nastyass as they are nutsycakes! And what's more, they totally remind me of my chiropractor, Steve, back on the Upper East Side on that tiny island known as Manhattan! Steve had the same eyes and cheeks—and, well, yes, was a bit bearish, as well! Oh my God, I hope he doesn't read this! Moving on. This . . . is Steve—shit—I mean: This . . . is the wombat.

Oh, my sweet Lord, this li'l Aussie baby is begging for a belly tickle while sunbathing!

I'm gonna bite that ass If you don't hurry up and move it!

says this rascally pup to the wombat!

FYI: Though native to Australia, they're rarely seen. This could be because their species is in **critical danger**. Since so many dwell in Tasmania, they often fall prey to the nastyass Tasmanian devil and wild dingo. What with that and crazy diseases and nastyass shit introduced by farmers to the wombat's habitat, it's a blessing they're only at the critical level. Zoos, wombat reserves, and conservation groups are helping to protect these furry li'l teddy bears.

MARSUPIAL HERBIVORES, WOMBATS LOVE TO chomp carrots, chew grass and graze in the wee hours while Australia sleeps. They are generally about 40 inches long and 50 to 60 pounds on the scale. They digest their vegetation, like, super slowly. We're talking sometimes up to, like, two weeks—just to digest some shit! How crazy! Likewise, they tend not to move very fast. They spend a great deal of time digging and burrowing, but when it comes to moving around, you can forget about wombats joining any speed-walking groups at the mall!

> One step closer and I may have to barrel into you, stupid!

says Steve—
I mean, the wombat!

BUT, JUST WHEN YOU THOUGHT they're all cute and squeezable, along come stories of wombat attacks! That's right, stupid, sometimes—when humans and wombats cross, strange shit happens. As a defense mechanism, they will go for it and run at top speed into you to knock you down and start chomping on your face! They'll turn into li'l furry bowling balls and just fucking plow right into you! That's quite a lot of moxie from such precious li'l furry babies, no?

> I'm gonna eat your face!

THESE NOCTURNAL GUINEA PIGS on steroids have little sharp teeth that are forever growing. How crazy! They wear them down by chewing on bark and shit like that. While they prefer to live alone with their neuroses, sometimes wombats will colonize and have bake sales for the betterment of their burrowed communities.

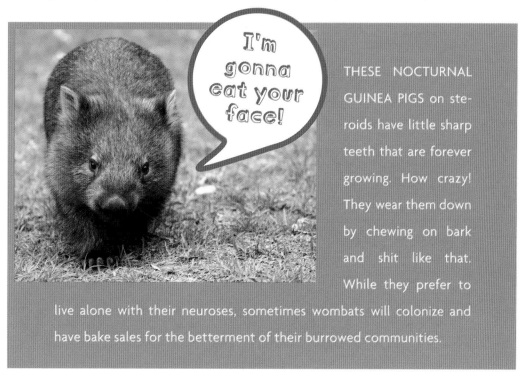

THESE MAMMALS CAN DIG BURROWS as long as 100 feet! I wasn't fibbin' when I told you how much they enjoy burrowing and digging. They even create tunnel systems and underground compounds!

Wombats generally have a nice long life. Provided they avoid disease, don't become prey to dingoes, and steer clear of the farmers who fuck with them, they'll live up to 30-plus years!

All right, Mr. DeMille, I'm ready for my close-up and some clumps of grass!

They are protected animals and, therefore, illegal to sneak off and domesticate. You really wouldn't want to, anyway, as they can be superaggressive and eat your face! In fact, they're so badass, they can bust through just about anything: doors, walls, sofas, and so on. So, please, by the next paragraph, try to stop thinking about owning an adorable wombat as a pet.

Wombat poo, or "scat," supposedly has a fragrance all its own! *Ewwww!* Who the hell is going around sniffing wombat poops? That is so heinous. First, my dreams are shattered when I learn I can't own one because they're too fucking crazy and bitey, then I find out they're face eaters, and now this? Stinky scat poops! It's a lot to take in all at once, I know. Believe me, I wasn't expecting all of this from the pudgy li'l Aussie teddy baby, either.

LIKE A FEW OTHER NASTYASS ANIMALS in this book, the wombat, which generally likes to fly solo, will occasionally shack up with a mate and raise a family. Wombats become sexually active at around three years old. The females tend to give birth to their babies in the fall through spring. When the babies are born (the size of peas!), they find their way to the mama's marsupium and will chill there until confident enough to make it in the real world on their own. And, interesting to note, the pouches are upside down, but the baby wombies don't fall out! Another interesting fact? The females have two vaginas . . . there, I said it!

There are times when a young wombat will feel scared and dive back into its mama's pouch, just until its panic attack passes. But by the time it's fully grown, the notion of hopping back into the pouch has become a thing of the past. Yesterday's tuna.

'I'm gettin' way too old for mama's pouch.'

NOW, HERE'S SOMETHING ABOUT WOMBATS that I absolutely love: how they sleep. Mostly they'll sleep on their backs with their little feeties in the air. Sometimes, though, they'll curl up like little sleepy babies. Either way, they sleep like humans, which is just so adorable! I know, I know. "Randall, you can't have a wombat." OK. Fine. I get it. (But they're sooo chubby and cute!)

THE AMERICAN BULLFROG

(Li'l bully)

GET READY TO LOOK AT the American bullfrog in a whole new way. OK? You have been warned. I'm being very cereals! For starters, American bullfrogs—or, as I like to call them, "li'l bullies"—hold the title as North America's largest frogs. So instantly when I think of them, I think of schoolyard bullies, bullies in karate class, bullies in the workplace. Bully, bully, bully! God, I sound like Teddy Roosevelt!

Human bullies suck, and at the end of the day, are the ones who really need therapy! There's simply no logical fucking reason to torture and bully someone. I just hope anyone who is or has ever been bullied understands that bullies are the ones who need serious help! So, screw bullies—they seriously need to get their own lives straightened out, as well as focus on bettering and loving themselves! I have no tolerance for bullying. Period.

Animal bullies, on the other paw, are just nasty! These li'l American bullies are just such crrrazy amphibians! They're pretty hefty. Hefty and scary. You think I'm nuts, but I'm telling you—they're nothing like the friendly, talking, and dancing frogs you see on television. Not even close, stupid!

This chef cooks up **everything** from birds to-other bullies . . . nasty!!!

AMERICAN BULLFROGS ARE CANNIBALS. If hungry enough, they will eat their friends—they totally do not give a shit. If bully's hungry, bully eat! They'll snack on birds, bats, insects, rodents, scorpions, snakes, and, quite literally, anything else with a pulse. How nasty that they eat one another, right?! I mean, how the hell can they live with themselves? I think, perhaps in this case, the li'l bullies' tummies are way larger than their consciences!

If I could, I would eat myself!

SADLY, IN ADDITION TO HAVING their dead bodies dissected in practically every high school throughout the United States, American bullfrogs are also consumed by millions each year. People claim they're delish, but I would never, ever try eating one. That's just grossy! My friend Fernando constantly tries to sell me on eating snails and frogs. And I'm always like, "Hells no, honey!"

WHEN I WAS YOUNGER, I would run around and collect frogs and then let them all run loose from my sand pail. I always thought they were cool, until I got older and learned the ugly truth about their nastyass cannibalistic habits and meanass ways of drowning their prey in their mouths! Yuck, though . . . I must admit, kinda genius, no? I mean, to have the tenacity to pull a live animal into the water and then swallow it? Good gravy, that's just too shocking! They could have eaten me when I was a boy collecting them to release them! Oh dear!

Holy shit! Did that li'l bully just eat a fucking bird?! It did! Oh my, sweet noodles!!!

TO ATTRACT MATES, LI'L BULLIES have a crazy call they like to use, which is loud and guttural. So loud, in fact, it can be heard by everyone within a half-mile radius! Jesus! They get their names, actually, from this nutty, bassy, rolling call, because folks believed they sounded like bulls! Ha! If only they knew how *way* more terrifying these li'l bullies are than bulls.

fact-tastic:

American bullfrogs can be found in the "hot spots" of the United States. Years are added to the li'l bullies' lives when they live in warm environments. They're mostly pond and lake dwellers, and can grow to three to six inches! Yikes!

Don't even think 'bout it, stupid!

NOCTURNAL BY NATURE, THE LI'L bullies have spread to some parts of Canada, as well as to the West Coast in the United States. They can totally be kept as pets as long as they're cared for and given the proper environment. In fact, frogs always make great pets, as do turtles! Just don't get a rodent or bird and put it near the bully!

Let's face it, stupid,
kind of nasty.

Q. **"BUT WAIT, RANDALL, HOW DO THE LI'L BULLIES MAKE TADPOLES?" YOU ASK.**

A. Great question! The male rides on top of the female and then the female gets excited and releases all of her eggs (sometimes nearly 20,000 of them!) into the water. At the same time (hopefully) the male gets excited, too, and releases his spermys into the water, as well. The "making tadpoles" process takes place all outside of the parents' bodies! Isn't that something? "Bullfrog porn" was popular in the late '40s for some reason. Lots of naughty films and old black-and-white snapshots—but there's not so much interest in frog porn these days, even with the Internet! Go figure. Eggs usually hatch in no time (a few days) and then, in their own time, li'l bullies morph from tadpoles to bullfrogs! How exciting! Before you know it, baby'll be killing crazy shit and eating it!

OVER TIME, AMERICAN BULLIES were introduced to other countries, including Brazil, parts of Europe, Australia, and Colombia. This li'l bully went and fucked up their ecologies by eating all sorts of crazy shit! Well, duh! What were you thinking? Did you think you could just introduce a nastyass American species to your country and not expect any changes to your natural food chain?! So stupid!

What's hoppin'? I'm just chillin' in my B-Frog stance.

AS NASTY AS THESE LI'L BULLY amphibians may be, they have a certain swagger to them, don't they? It's as though they are fully aware of their strength in numbers. Like, "You can eat as many of us as you want and cut us apart in all of your schools, but we'll still be here, stupid!" And that's no joke! Every late spring through early summer, these bullies reproduce and keep the species strong. I guess this is why they feel they can take the nasty liberty of just eating each other. What the—am I actually trying to justify amphibious cannibalism? Nastyyy!

THE SLOTH

(Sloooooooowwwwwwass cutie)

THIS . . . IS THE SLOOOOOOOOWWWWWWASS SLOTH! And let me start by saying that even though they are always late for dinner and take forever to show up to anything you invite them to, they are so sweet and good-natured! They are special mammals that have been around for fucking ever, like, 50 million–plus years. Yeah! These slowwwww sloths can be found throughout Central and South American jungles and rain forests. You should know, there are two-toed sloths and three-toed sloths. So, next time you have to go shopping for sandals with a sloth, take that into consideration.

Of the six different species of sloth, one is **endangered** and another is **critically endangered**. Both are of the three-toed variety and dwell in Brazil. There are sloth sanctuaries that do a wonderful job protecting and caring for them. Some sloths end up in zoos, where they live like slowass rock stars and are a huge hit with young and old visitors alike!

"When I wake up, I'm-a eat all these leaves and have breakfast in bed again!"

SLOTHS ARE NOCTURNAL, and are perfectly capable of finding a perfect treetop to call home and staying there for years! The only time they'll really move around is to take weekly poops (which, FYI, are always in the same spot)! That's it! They find no other reason to come down. Sadly, when they do, they run the risk of getting lost and winding up in some sort of danger—be it from electricity poles or cars! Please be careful, sloth! When safe and sound, sloths can generally live a little over 30 years! If they booze it up every day, chain-smoke, and try to assimilate, they'll live a week! They truly spend most of their lives just chillaxin' up in the trees, swinging around and looking cute! They'll sleep upside down for nearly nine to ten hours! Holy shit! Now, this is a mammal that really knows how to take its time and relax!

What's that, Sandy? You want to talk? Hold on, I'll come over to you—just give me 14 hours, and I'll be right there!

Actually, should a sloth ever encounter a predator, it will most likely take soft swipes at it with its longass, crazy claws. Those claws are sharp and essentially serve as big grappling hooks. So they do have that form of defense . . . in addition to telling longass, boring stories that go nowhere slowly! But they'll only do this when in some serious danger!

LISTEN, HANGIN' AROUND UPSIDE DOWN off of branches is something these sloths are very used to—in fact, they're born upside down! Yeah, can you believe that shit?! Surprisingly, when sloths have sex, it does not take three years—it actually occurs in real time. It's just the foreplay that takes eons!

Mama sloths will give birth upside down and the babies are expected to just—you know—figure gravity out right then and there! The sweet smiling sloth babies will stay with their mamas until they feel confident enough to sleep nine hours and take slow poop trips on their own. Big cats seem to be their main predator. And, unfortunately, once on the ground, if a sloth should come face to face with, say, a jag, it's not like it'll quickly run up a tree! Poor slothy! Hurry and poop!

Well, guys, I've had a **great time tonight**, but it's gonna take me awhile to get home, so . . .

SLOTHS EAT LEAVES. DUH! OBVI! But they also love to snack on fruits and an occasional insect or even a bird! But they mostly stick to the leaves. Their digestive system works at a snail's pace—thus, the weekly poops. No jokes! Sloths' tummies won't break down the leaves and raw twigs for at least a whole month! Meanwhile, the leaves provide no nutritional value whatsoever, nor do they provide any energy! Sloths' muscles are like fabulous loose strings or ribbons! If you challenged a sloth to an arm-wrestling match, you'd not only win, but you'd also be such an asshole!

THE SLOWASS SLOTH HAS AN amazingly fabulous fur coat, which, contrary to most mammals', features hairs that grow away from its limbs because of all the dangling from trees it does! Isn't that crazy?!

"Whoops! I just dropped my brush! Shit, that'll take at least a week to get back!"

Not as crazy as this sloth secret I have to share with you. Ready? All sloths really have three toes! The "two-toed" sloth just refers to the fact it has two fingers on its hands. But who am I to change its name suddenly . . . after all this time? Please, keep this secret to yourself!

Here's my assistant, Chrissy Flowerbottoms, with a nine-month-old baby sloth! What a precious li'l munchkin! I am so jellybeans he got to hold a baby sloth! Shit!

STUPID POACHERS NEED TO LEAVE these slowass babies alone. This is another problem with being a slowass—peeps can just up and take you! How disgusting is that? To just take an innocent animal right out of its environment? Oh, please—who am I kidding? It's just another case to add to the large pile of animal injustices. But I am hopeful that, together, we can all do more to fully respect and love all of the animals we share this planet with. Like the fabulous Mahatma Gandhi said, "The greatness of a nation and its moral progress can be judged by the way its animals are treated."

fact-tastic:

Sloths are just so fascinating, and cute as hell! Their eyesight is extremely poor, as is their hearing. This is probably for the best, as I'm sure they get plenty of angry comments from other animals, trying to pass them in the trees. Monkeys are all, "Will you please hurry your slowass up, stupid?" And sloths are like, "I'm sorry, sweetie, what'd you say? I'm a bit slow today!"

PHOTO CREDITS

PHOTO RESEARCH: Meg Handler

PHOTO CREATIONS: Teri Elefante/Absolute Perfection Graphics & Design/ www.absoluteperfectiondesign.com

P. ii: Nick Garbutt/NPL/Minden Pictures

P. iv: honey badger, Getty Images; aye-aye, bullfrog, tarsier, wombat, SuperStock; solenodon, Ardea; armadillo, Mariella Superina; opossum, David Seerveld; emperor tamarin, Ethan Fisher; Tasmanian devil, Nature Picture Library; sloth, Minden Pictures.

Ardea: P. 19, 22 (top), 47, 48

Auscape International: P. 18, 20 (top)

Gerald Cubitt: P. viii

Eladio Fernandez: P. 53

Guillermo Ferraris: P. 29, 30 (top)

Ethan Fisher: P. 24–27

FLPA—Images of Nature: P. 10 (top)

Getty Images: P. 7 (top), 55, 56, 59, 60, 62 (2), 64 (2), 65 (2)

David Knowles: P. 1, 9 (bottom)

Minden Pictures: P. vii, 5, 6, 7 (bottom), 10 (bottom), 11, 54, 58, 66–70

Naples Zoo at Caribbean Gardens: P. 2, 4, 8, 9 (top), 71

Nature Picture Library: P. 13, 16 (top), 17 (top), 20 (bottom), 21, 22 (bottom), 23 (bottom)

NHPA.co.uk: P. 16 (bottom)

Dr. Jose Nuñez-Miño/ www.thelastsurvivors.org: P. 46, 49–52

OSF Images: 23 (top)

The Neal Peters Collection: P. 13

PhotoLibrary.com: P. 17 (bottom)

PhotoShot: P. 14 (2)

David Seerveld: P. 40–45

Mariella Superina: P. 28, 30 (bottom), 31

SuperStock: P. 12, 15, 32, 34–39, 57 (2), 63

Bennie van Zyl: P. 3